Love Notes Life Notes

Douglas Schueler

Copyright © 2007 by Douglas Schueler

Love Notes Life Notes
by Douglas Schueler

Printed in the United States of America

ISBN 978-1-60266-289-6

All rights reserved solely by the author. The author guarantees all contents are original and do not infringe upon the legal rights of any other person or work. No part of this book may be reproduced in any form without the permission of the author. The views expressed in this book are not necessarily those of the publisher.

www.xulonpress.com

The Journey

Body, mind and soul
Down the road we go

As one we have control
And along the path we'll roll

Excitement is the key
Follow us and see

With inner peace of mind
Show love and being kind

True faith will lead you through
All treasures come to you

Seek power from above
And receive His holy love

The man who seeks success
Knows knowledge is the best

Fulfill your dreams you might
If you follow His holy light

All time your gift will be
Throughout eternity

With body, mind and soul
Down the road we'll go

You'll Make It

It may look high and rough to go
But don't you fret just take it slow

Go hand over hand one step at a time
And you'll reach the top just follow the sign

Just keep your eyes looking straight ahead
Don't look back focus your mind instead

Your dreams are there for you to reach
He gives the power to all of those who seek

The rocks are loose and may cause a fall
But don't give up just stand up tall

Dust yourself off and try it again
For when it's all over you will laugh and grin

Happiness forever will be your prize
Just keep heading towards the clouds and into the skies

The lightning may strike and the thunder boom
But just beyond these may your destiny loom

Don't give up it may be only one more step
Between you and the top of which your goals were set

So push yourself on and up to your limit
And don't worry 'bout a thing because I know
You'll Make It

Within His Sight

Within His Sight I'll always be
Throughout all my life all eternity

His light I'll follow the straight path I'll go
True devotion and Faith is what I'll show

Within His arms with peace and love
My heart I give without reserve, above

I thank Him much day in day out
His will I chose no regret or doubt

Patience, humbleness, and obedience shown
With honor, adoration my strength has grown

He holds out his hands to welcome one and all
Gives council and guidance so I will not fall

When my spirits are low and I feel somewhat down
His words I hear to warm my heart, reverse my frown

True wisdom then will I understand and gain
To keep me safe from evil and never-ending pain

Praise and love I return in kind
So everlasting life I will someday find

Within His Sight I'll always be
Throughout all my life all eternity

Our Destiny

Lord of Light, Lord of night, Lord of wondrous gifts,
Lord so loving, so generous, so kind,
one's spirit He always lifts.

To one, to all He spreads His Light each and every day,
To brighten our lives and lead us on,
our Lord He is the way.

Wisdom, Knowledge,
Understanding-all are given of those who look,
All written down for us to read and live in His big book.

Each and every passage inscribed has life within Its lines,
To lead us to our destiny like grapes growing on the vines.

So strength and courage are given to us
when we remain in touch,
Remember His ways and praise His name,
He gives us all so much.

Yes, Jesus loves me, this I know, each day He tells me so,
As I spread His message of Love and Hope
everywhere I go.

Harmony and Peace abound for those who hear His call,
No wants or needs are lacking,
for His love has filled them all.

One people gathered in His midst, united with a cause,
To find the lost and suffering and give them
reason to pause.

Just take the time to think of Him before your day begins,
Because with Jesus Christ the Living Light
each one of us wins.

So remember,
The Light is there for us to see and guide us on our path,
To lead us to His Kingdom above for the gifts,
for us He hath.

A Love Letter

Dear Lord,
Your ominous Power excites my heart and soul,
No worries or fears do I have as I know You are in control.

This Mystery we call Life with its every twist and turn,
Is but a flicker in time to You but is still of Your concern.

Ages ago and ages to come Your mighty Hand
points out our way,
With guidance from above to lead us to that final day.

With Your great Knowledge,
Wisdom and Understanding we learn to know,
That without You in our lives there is no place else to go.

Your great Love for us is never ending
and is beyond our belief,
And every day I think of You leads me
to happiness and away from grief.

Your miraculous ways amaze the simple who live
without preparation,
But as I watch You I begin to learn of Your plans
for our Salvation.

Your awesome Presence is a sign before me as
my life to you I raise,
This generous gift You give me is more the reason
Your Name I praise.

The dreams and desires I possess are from
Your vast supply of endless graces,
To be granted unto me through my daily diligence,
patience and smiling faces.

For You, the Mighty Lamb upon the throne,
watch over my labor and shepherd me,
Neither hunger nor thirst nor heat of the sun
upon me shall there be.

And so, as Your Ominous Power daily
excites my heart and soul,
No worries or fears do I have as I know
You are in control.

Just Dream

Stretch your thinking, open your mind,
Anything you imagine, any shape, any kind.

Visions of your eye, but yet seen not,
A bright shining light, that never grows hot.

Follow through faith, with out-stretched hand,
This path of faint footsteps, no matter the demand.

Clouds may come, dense fog fill the sky,
Just focus your vision, think of the Why!

Persistency pays, as is patience a must,
When the fog and clouds lift, you stand tall in the dust.

Your destination clear, only a short distance to go,
Stay strong with your efforts,
and with consistence it'll show.

As the journey at hand, draws close to its ends,
Once small dreams grow ever larger,
and your next goal begins.

Territory never traveled, a new shining light to seek out,
As ever onward you follow, with faith there's no doubt.

As you take the lead, mind focused on unknown shores,
Many will follow in footsteps,
that have now become yours.

So continue expanding your mind,
as possibilities never cease,
Dreams were made to be fulfilled,
as one's life they increase.

Friendship Is

Friendship means the world to me,
It lasts throughout Eternity.

Friendship knows no bound, it has no limit,
People sharing themselves, and their talents within it.

Friendship gives of itself, asking no return in kind,
The most wonderful of feelings, everyone should find.

Friendship hears in deep silence, the cries of the lost,
It reaches out arms to give help, no matter the cost.

Friendship holds dear the late nights,
when we grow so near,
It brings life into reach, to help calm every fear.

Friendship shows its true inner self, without regret,
It's the times to cherish, and never forget.

Friendship understands the past, but the future it sees,
It has hope for the weary, like a cool summer breeze.

Friendship strengthens our souls, so ever onward we go,
To find others in need, for our own mercy to show.

Friendship brings each one, and all to reach out,
To spread cheer and happiness, this is no doubt.

Friendship comes from where else, but Heaven above,
Friendship my dear, Friendship is Pure Love.

The Path of Life

The Path of Life leads into the Light,
Through clouds of darkness and into His sight.

Though obstacles are many as you go on your way,
They test your character each and every day.

Your strength and courage build as you go,
Till changes occur that outwardly show.

Intensity, understanding and wisdom abound,
And soon draw crowds that gather around.

Knowledge you teach to those who will learn,
You tell them the News and give them a burn.

Deep inside the News spreads throughout,
Till action is taken because there's no doubt.

So they start on the Path seeking the Light,
While along by their side you walk through the night.

As obstacles come as surly they do,
You lend a hand to help them get through.

As strength and courage in them increase,
You point out the way and their hand you release.

The Path of Life they're on leads into the Light,
Through the darkest of clouds into His sight.

Focus On The Father

Looking up to Heaven, for answers and advice,
One should Focus on the Father, to do the best in Life.

No matter where one is headed, or what is on one's mind,
The journey should be together, not alone, as one will find.

A single soul can travel, a distance for a while,
But without the help and guidance, confusion starts to pile.

When one's focus tends to drift, and the obstacles
grow fiercer,
The road ahead just lengthens, and despair comes
ever nearer.

On the verge of breakdown, all hope seems lost for good,
Until an inner voice long lost, rings out – If only I could.

A glimmer of light shines through the dark, its strength
grows ever brighter,
In time with trust and letting go, the load grows
even lighter.

Reaching out one's hand, and giving the burdens
of the Heart,
Relieves the soul of stress and worry, one receives
a brand new start.

As maturity and growth advance, one's eyes begin to open,
A whole new world appears ahead, a whole new journey
is taken.

No longer alone does one go on, all obstacles seem smaller,
An inner peace and faith exists, one's trust grows in
the Father.

All answers and advice are there, in Heaven for those
who seek,
So, Focus on the Father each day, He makes life strong
from those once weak.

Tragedy?

Was it a real Tragedy or really just a trial?
Was there an impression made or only last a while?

Obstacles abound in Life to challenge you and me,
Attitude creates the flow to Success or Tragedy.

How you travel through your course is up to you to go,
Tragedy will be your lot without the work you show.

A goal set firm to show you why helps for you to see,
A path to travel, destination known, you miss –
not Tragedy.

Faith in Dreams, yet to be seen, comes to those who wait,
Give up to soon, turn away, Tragedy slams shut the gate.

Strength, you know, comes from above,
to drive you to your goal,
God's the one to whom to seek,
Tragedy's from dice you roll.

No chance, no luck, 'cause Life's no game,
a Plan for each shines through,
The choice is ours, Free Will by name,
Success or Tragedy – you choose.

It's up to each to make up one's mind,
for our future we do create,
For Life goes on – a continuous climb – look back,
Tragedy's your fate.

Your Life could be a Tragedy if you allow it to pass by,
Learn your lesson, move on by Faith, your future
will be Blue Sky.

When there's an impression made,
the pain may last a while,
It will not be a real Tragedy, if you see it as just a trial.

The Puzzle

Many shapes, many sizes, many colors thrown as one,
All the same, yet many pieces, many features do they come.

The goal is there, connect the pieces,
use them all to form one whole,
The idea is simple, yet not easy,
where to start is your first role.

Plan your work around your goal, lay it out for you to see,
Then work your plan that you set forth,
with confidence, that is the key.

With dedication to your work, your effort brings success,
The pieces fit so easily, a shape comes from the mess.

As you continue to move on, confusion can set in,
Til what seemed once an easy task,
can make your head to spin.

Colors blend, shapes and sizes mix,
some pieces can be lost,
Self-image drops, confidence wanes –
Is it really worth the cost?

Value towards the goal that's sought,
is measured through your thought,
Weigh it well, don't guess your fate,
or all may be for naught.

Instructions you desire, are here for you to use,
They help you look within yourself,
and show you how to choose.

The Book is your example, to help complete your goal,
Follow its directions, and as the picture clears,
resume your role.

The goal is reached, the puzzle complete,
your life has been laid down,
Then the final piece of the puzzle is set,
when you receive His Crown.

The Torch

Down deep in a lost Heart, like a vast, cold, dank cave,
One's feelings are sunken, one knows not how to behave.

The shadows of happiness, they are hidden or not there,
This poor Heart is wondering, "Does anyone care?"

Reaching to feel, for a way to get out,
Unless help comes soon, Hope turns into doubt.

Far off in the darkness, a Light pierces through,
So tiny at first sight, is it the mind or is it true?

The farther the Heart goes, shapes come into form,
As the Light grows much stronger, one feels kind of warm.

The Heart opens itself, it goes up to the Light,
It catches a spark, and begins to burn at the sight.

With the burning Heart's hope, and happiness renewed
and restored,
It goes back to the darkness, with strength from the Lord.

In search of other lost Hearts, as memory recalls,
The burning Heart's desire, to help those sunken from
their falls.

The burning Heart's light, pierces into the dark,
Until it comes to a lost Heart, and lends it a spark.

The darkness surrounding the Hearts, grows much lighter,
As the Light of the World, like a Torch, burns ever brighter.

The Cliff

As you're heading through life alone, 100 miles an hour,
You think you are right and safe, like a king in his tower.

All the turns you take, no matter which way you go,
Appear to move you higher up, there's no reason
for you to slow.

You're heading towards your peak, all "luck" seems
on your side,
Everyone around draws close, and works to keep in stride.

But no advice you take from those, you'll make it
on your own,
As you continue on your "self-made" path, there's a danger
to you unknown.

With no guide to lead you through, a wrong road do you
now take,
But blinded by your own sure self, you don't see your
big mistake.

Seeing where you are headed, those around will show
they care,
But your mind is set, you turn away, only to their despair.

Now at "the top" of your ascent, alone in "victory"
your hand you lift,
Admiring yourself you fail to see, you've headed off a cliff.

As down you fall you reach out for help, to find a place
to hold,
All hope starts to fade and despair sets in, till you recall
advice you've been told.

To seek council and advice in life, you need friends to help you stand,
You take heed of this thought, you stretch yourself out, you take another's hand.

And now lifted up by those around, you set your sight on new goals,
Your new life's journey begins among others, to pull from The Cliff other lost souls.

Looking Within From Without

Standing at the mirror, looking on with so much doubt,
A poor souls happiness has left it, because it's looking only from without.

For many years the soul looked on, but witnessed only sorrow,
Not knowing deep inside itself, the potential of a new tomorrow.

The value the soul placed on itself, with no guide to choose its fate,
Was so far below the zero mark, it felt worthless, "It's too late."

With overwhelming fear built up, and "No one can help me now,"
The poor soul seemed lost forever, a way to save it, it wondered "How?"

The thoughts that no one really cared, or even heard its cry,
Shot like arrows deep into its heart, the soul nearly gave up its will to try.

As down the soul began to fall, its life it felt it would loose,
Another soul stepped up to help, and showed it a way to choose.

The new soul appeared very happy, and took the souls attention somewhat aback,
But refreshing the words that were spoken, they seemed to be right on track.

At first their sound was to be foreign, the soul knew not
which way to react,
Until the new soul looked into its eyes, and told the soul
one simple fact.

The way to truly be happy, one must look inside its soul
and show its Love,
It's a joy to give out to the world, it is Power from
Heaven above.

As now in its travels the soul goes, to spread its Love now
that there's no doubt,
It shows others misguided as it was, how to Look Within
themselves From Without.

God's Love

God's Divine, Eternal Plan was to create a World of Love,
To present a Gift of Life to all, He sent these from Heaven above.

Each man and woman and child created, for each to come together,
In peace and harmony and friendship all, one body to live forever.

To bring us close He sent us words of wise, to guide us to His Glory,
Many carried these thoughts, laid down for us all, and given in a Book or Story.

We ask for what we need from Him, to help make our lives complete,
Working hand in hand each one helps out, our desires He can thus meet.

Our goals, our Dreams, our future He knows, He guides us along our path,
When we open our Hearts and let Him in, He shows us the Love He hath.

Our understanding and ways not His, but our Faith thus leads us through,
When we trust in His sight, believe in Him true, and make it our own sight too.

And as farther along in our Life we go, and clearer our eyes do see,
We view how we too can take hold of His Love, and spread it around like did He.

The people we reach and whose lives we touch, become a link in a chain,
That spreads through the world to bind us as one, to help overcome our trials and pain.

These Fires of Life help our strength to grow, although they seem hard to us at the time,
They remind us of God's greatest Gift of Love, that He sent His Son Who laid His life on the line.

So this Gift of Life He gave to us all, that was sent from Heaven above,
Was God's Divine, Eternal Plan for us, to create a World of Love.

The Wall

Impressionistic, pliable, a Young Life begins to form,
Not knowing what is right or wrong, its surroundings set the norm.

Learning from those who guide and teach, the Young Life reacts in turn,
An open book set to be filled, for knowledge does it thus yearn.

The information comes in time, and with excitement the Young Life drinks it in,
Like a refreshing glass of water, but not always knowing what's contained within.

The taste of some information seems great, but unbeknownst to the Young Life,
Mixed signals sent on how to act, begin to create a path towards strife.

Understanding can become lost in a mist, and clouds of confusion mount up so tall,
The Young Life's view of how to live and be safe, creates a self-protection or a wall.

Moving away from things that "burn", and shutting itself off from the world,
The Young Life goes deeper within itself, into an existence of loneliness is it thus hurled.

Far away and out of touch, there seems to be no turning back or help in sight,
As depression sets in to take its toll, the Young Life starts to slip from the Light.

But just before the "light goes out", a glimmer of Hope
shines through the dark,
An almost blinding sight, as the Young Life sees a hand,
helps create a fire from a spark.

The hand of a Friend pulls it up to its feet, and begins to
show it the way,
As the Young Life learns the Truth, on how it should live,
the clouds soon clear to a bright sunny day.

The Truth of Life to learn, to tear down walls of fear and
doubt, or to keep from having them start,
A Young Life should be taught and know, Jesus Christ died
for all, and to keep Him deep within our heart.

Time Lapse

Ages past, ages to come, and the age we live in today,
Time stands still, but yet it goes on, we'd like for some to stay.

Our lives are linked with this time as one, as we seek to interpret our path,
The way we choose, as life goes on, will determine the rewards we will hath.

Most live their lives in yesterday's eyes, they're blind to what's in store,
They see what once was, as if it still is, stop looking and close the door.

Their time capsules are grand, and many look on, in total awe at the show,
But interest does wane, as hours pass by, and soon they have to go.

Their lives are filled with, "I want it all now," their past is laid waste behind,
As they live for the moment, and want it to last, they miss much more than they find.

Once today is lost, tomorrow slips into its place, the cycle begins again,
And they're caught in the here and the now takes hold, their future comes on a whim.

Their futures are bright as they plan and set goals, life is wide open to them,
As not a day will go by, no hour laid waste, good gifts are the fruit that will stem.

Their past they remember, but only to launch a new shoot,
their tree of life never stops,
As the sky is their limit, they continue to grow, because
they've removed all the tops.

Just remember in life to look up for advice, whichever
direction you may plan,
Or it will be for naught, without truth and help, direct from
the Great I AM.

Your time is a gift, waste none if you can, your free will
helps you go forward in life,
Then your ages will come, and your ages will go, and you
can live today with no worry or strife.

Nature's Best

Unquestionable beauty surrounds one east and west,
A marvel to behold it all it's known as Nature's Best.

As one begins along the trail the way is smooth and clear,
One's eyes are on the marvels ahead and sees no need to fear.

The beauty of one's travels cover each bend that one goes round,
But farther on the journey one's paths go up and down.

Each step into the future one finds challenges untold,
As occasionally downed limbs appear or a decision - a fork in the road.

Discernment brings with it questions of which direction is best to go,
Does one trust in self and choose the way or allow another to show?

As others come along one's path much advise is one thus given,
But it's still up to one to decide to choose as it's one's life one is livin'.

As one sifts through the messages the facts and truths are weighed,
The best trail to follow seems easier as travel plans are made.

Trail plans through life become simple and the direction is easy to see,

When one follows advice from "Life's Trail Guide" one
will go where one needs to be.

One's journey begins to show that many trails through life
are for naught,
As one hears advice on what truth is and should've learned
or been taught.

So, enjoy the beauty of Nature's Best that surrounds you on
your way,
But follow the trail of the Creator who fashioned it with
each new day.

Sweet Love

In the arms of the Father we begin our wonderful lives,
We hold close to His warmth of His Sweet Love gives us our drives.

As we leave from His side our goal is made clear,
We are sent to give joy and Sweet Love to those here.

As babies new born we're gifts to be cherished, held and adored,
So precious and innocent we're the physical Sweet Love straight from the Lord.

So small we begin we depend on our parents for help and for growth,
The Sweet Love we give them they return back as an oath.

We're taught to be friends and be kind to all of man,
To spread our Sweet Love to as many as we can.

While we grow in His Knowledge we extend blessings to all,
We reach out our arms of Sweet Love so others don't fall.

We catch those we can and help them press on to their Dreams,
Our Sweet Love we express shows them life is more than it seems.

We were created and placed here to be a light in the dark like a beacon,
To unite our Sweet Love and show others it's the Father they're seekin'.

So together we travel to all places about,
To spread our Sweet Love and extinguish the doubt.

Then one day together we'll enter with many others above,
In the arms of the Father to be held close to His warmth
and Sweet Love.

In His Step

Our lives are but a shadow in time, as brief as a day is long,
We need to make the most we're given, to continue our way and be strong.

The burdens encountered will try our souls, they may bring us to our knees,
But great people of past were made, from struggles and heartaches such as these.

To be broken and weak is strength to those, who decide that alone they can't go,
Though not in man's eyes, but the One in the skies, who wants our hearts to grow.

When we try it ourselves and see it our way, our paths become jumbled and thick,
We end up on our face all bruised and alone, our souls suffer and we become sick.

So, when on our knees we can't stand by ourselves, hope seems lost and we feel so inept,
That's when our arms should reach up, our voices raise high and we look to walk In His Step.

For the path of Our Father is made for us all, His footprints are plain to see,
Our lives will be better, our heartaches made softer, when we strive like Him to be.

And though walls may rise to close us inside, and fire heat up at our door,
No fear shall we have as we're never alone, we just call on the Name of the Lord.

Like thunder He'll come and lightning He'll strike, those once failing to believe will see,
That if they trust and have faith, they too can be safe, both now and through eternity.

Your love should be spread to all you approach, and ask to join you on His path,
Since your life is a great creation, not to be buried, but to show what's inside your heart that you hath.

So, because our lives are so brief as a shadow, like each day we are come and we pass,
Remain In His Step, be strong on your way, and in His arms you will end up at last.

The Gift

Across the ages, throughout time itself, man has searched
both high and low,
Looking for something to ease his pain, to make Life easier
for which to go.

The trials encountered are burdens to most, and pull so
many down,
But easy solutions seem close at hand, they appear to be
all around.

The answers aren't clear, a quick fix so near, and many
are drawn aside,
Till they're trapped in a loop, an unending wave, and
they're carried away by the tide.

They're washed out to sea, they're tossed to and fro, they
appear to be getting ahead,
Not knowing the danger, so far from their Home, they're
deeper in trouble instead.

Months may pass, years go on by, before they see where
they've gone,
When one day they look round and no one is near by, they
seem to be all alone.

As fear sets in, when all hope seems to fade, will they ever
again see the shore?
Then a still small Voice, rings out in the night, "You'll not
be alone anymore!"

It starts like a whisper, sounds blown by the wind, is it real or just in their mind?
The closer they search, the louder it gets, but it's not around them they soon will find.

The exterior images will all fade away, and in their Life not play as big a part,
When they learn the answers are spoken directly, where else, but into their Heart.

Solutions come from above, to help us through Life, to guide us on our way,
So be still and listen, to the One Who knows, just how to brighten our day.

He speaks to us daily, if we're open to hear, our spirits He'll always lift,
He guides us through Life, He eases our pain, His Love is the Ultimate Gift.

Freedom

Wrapped up in this old world so tight, most all that go on through,
See themselves as something great, all others should look up to.

Look at me, I should go first, my work's the best of all,
Their voices ring, with sounds so loud, they look so big and tall.

To the top, they climb so high, the world is theirs to take,
Not a worry, they seem to have, their tree no one can shake.

While time proceeds, they've reached the heights, the stress begins to show,
As the winds beneath, from those stepped on, begin to wail and blow.

Alone they stand, as storms rage on, the end seems close in sight,
As down they fall, both bruised and cut, a hand grabs out so tight.

Taking hold and looking 'round, to see who helped them out,
They see a kindly face look on, He is different, there is no doubt.

Compassion does flow out from His eyes, He knows how they could be,
Their past can be forgotten, their future is what He'll see.

No longer will chains that bound them tight, unto this
world's domain,
For they can put their trust in the Savior's care, alone they
will not remain.

His arms are opened wide to all, to love and see them
through,
He shows them how to work as one, to reach for those once
like them too.

And so, this world is made a better place, as they work in
one accord,
Bound as servants, to their fellow man, this True Freedom
is their reward.

The Cross

Amidst the world's great wonders abounding, our Life's great pleasures unfold,
We're presented daily with paths to go, to discover its riches untold.

There are two ways to choose, while traveling on, it is up to us to discern,
One narrow and crooked, the other wide and well lit, we are young and have much to learn.

Intrigued and excited, we're dazzled by the show, the narrow trail we ignore,
We're off to a world, we imagine so grand, we can't wait to set out and explore.

The start of the journey is more than enough, we ask, "What could be greater than this?",
As things of this world are easy to get, and when young are hard to resist.

But as time lingers on and age takes its toll, our eyes will begin to see,
What once was all gold, becomes tarnished and rough, and isn't what we thought it would be.

Discouraged and worn, our lives seem like a waste, we're disgusted at our own sight,
Till we round the next bin, and see up ahead, what appears to be some sort of Light.

As closer we go, we realize we're back, we again have two
ways we can choose,
But with knowledge and wisdom, and truth at our side, we
see on the narrow path we can't lose.

And though abundant twists and turns and small ledges
abound, we can keep a smile on our face,
Because we know with persistence and faith we'll get
through, combined with God's Amazing Grace.

For Life's great wonders will astound, and pleasures amaze,
and what we'll discover and see,
Is that Christ's Love for us all, is greater than riches, or
what the world can give will be.

So race towards the Mark, don't be weary and fall, ignore
the world's words of a loss,
And with joy and cheer, lay down your troubles and fears,
and kneel at the foot of
The Cross.

The Swamp

Driving down the road of Life, our way is straight, smooth and clear,
We're cruising through at sixty-five, we have few cares or fear.

The days breeze by so easy, our plans are sure at hand,
Like clockwork goals are reached and passed, so little do they demand.

As farther travel takes us on, we approach a point unknown,
We thought we had the course laid out, this sight is not our own.

A detour sign placed in our path, will take a longer route,
But we know better, a shorter way, of ourselves we have no doubt.

Off this road we dare to go, where no one's gone before,
Deep into the woods ahead, our driving now becomes a chore.

The trees close in, the trail is rough, it's difficult to see,
Till we reach a point, where we are stuck and never dreamed we'd be.

It came so fast, we aren't prepared, we tried to stop too late,
Right into a Swamp we drive, mud up to the hood and the tailgate.

Alone we sit, confused and lost, we cry for help out loud,
We were wrong, we know that now, we confess we
are too proud.

We reach into the glove box, and pull out the "Manual"
to read,
We place our truck in four-wheel drive, and soon we learn
we're freed.

In no time now we're back on the road, straight, smooth
and clear is our Life,
As our course is set, we're headed "Home", and we have
no more fear or strife.

In the Arms of My Father

In the Arms of My Father, unto this world I'm brought,
No cares or fears or worries exist, right here they are for naught.

His Love surpasses all I know, with Him I'll always be,
Beyond His reach I do not go, my being alone I do not see.

But as time goes by I venture out, a little to learn and explore,
With each trip I become more curious, and travel out just that much more.

The length I stay with Him goes down, by myself I feel so sure,
My thoughts and actions begin to stray, each day they become less pure.

Soon I find I never return, on my own I start to go,
So caught up in the world's smooth draw, I want to see what it has to show.

For a while it's great, new things to see and do I come across and find,
But before I can turn around, or realize, I'm caught all up in a bind.

From the beauty of the snares of Life, I've now become blinded and am lost,
All for one quick "sweet" simple moment, my own Life has become the cost.

As I spiral down from where I've climbed, apart my Life now falls,
I hear a voice come from the dark, it soothes my Heart as it calls.

Much time has passed since I've heard the words, they grow much stronger and clear,
It's my Father's Love that pierces the night, telling me He's always been here.

So, now as I travel through this world alone, or with others in a group together,
I will not fear or worry in Life, as I know I'll always be In the Arms of My Father.

Face the Sun

Each morning I look up in the sky, as I start out each new day,
I'm encouraged as I Face the Sun, it's brightness lights my way.

My daily course I've plotted out, I've laid my plans in line,
Each step is set, they lead me where, I know I'll be just fine.

Onward, upward, I do go, I'm sure I cannot fail,
The trust I've placed upon myself, "I've got the bull by the tail."

This mountain I've built extends far up, I've taken myself so high,
The world looks great, I've done so well, I can now sit back and sigh.

As I relax to enjoy my life, I soon find out I've slipped,
I'm headed down the other side, to and fro I have been flipped.

Banged and bruised I hit the ground, I'm disoriented and lost,
The price I've paid for working alone, my ruin seems like the cost.

I wander out in search of help, distressed, through this deep valley,
About to give in to despair, a voice rings out, "Allow Me."

I'm told we are all here for each other, alone we
should not be,
We were made to come together and work,
as one large family.

So I've learned my trust is not in me, as one we
are much better,
When we place our lives and joys in Whom else, but our
one and only Creator.

And now each morning as I look in the sky, now my day
starts out greater and more fun,
As I follow the brightness that leads me on my way, and
I'm encouraged as I
Face the Son.

The Hand

Life begins, a precious child, so small, so wondrous
and gifted,
The pureness of one's journey begins, in the Hand is one
thus lifted.

Rolling, crawling, the struggle is met, anticipating eyes
look on,
With the Hand outstretched, a first step, the moment will
soon be gone.

Following behind, as one goes on, the shoes seem
so big to fill,
But walking along, hand in Hand, it helps to flatten
each hill.

The pace increases, one wants to run, to go off
on one's own,
To see the sights, experience life, one lets go of the Hand
to roam.

One finds it's great, the space is vast, an endless array
of pleasure,
But soon one discovers, one's gone too far, one realizes the
Hand held the treasure.

Seeking, searching, one travels back, one hopes that it's not
been too long,
To locate the place, where one began, as the past memory
of the Hand grows strong.

But as struggles mount, frustration sets in, one starts to give up hope,
Fatigued by the journey, one's gone so far, will one find the Hand or the end of one's rope?

Down on one's knees, one finally does go, unable any longer to stand,
One feels a warm touch, on one's left shoulder, one looks and sees it's the Hand.

"My child," one hears. "why did you seek, so long and hard for Me there?"
"Your Life has been, in my Hand each day, I've overcome the world and its cares."

So remember one's Life, is a wondrous thing, a valuable gift that is precious,
A journey so great, if we only allow, our Creator's Hand to guide and to lift us.

The Choice

All through my life the way I will go, the choice it is up to me,
Though I think it's my own, "Am I in it alone?" the answer was hard to see.

I look to and fro', I see no one around, the choice I made was clear,
It cut like a whip, the words they were harsh, like hot coals each one did sear.

I said what I felt, no thought did I give, and the choice was black or white,
But the thorns they were sharp, they cut like a knife, they'd give a sane man a fright.

As if with no morals within, the choice to look and indulge, I gazed and took in the view,
The weight of the wood, the unbearable load, the splinters were razor sharp too.

My neighbor had plenty, that I did not, the choice I thought, "I want what he did own,"
Driven so hard, a crack was heard loud, the spikes they went straight through the bone.

What funds I acquired, no question or doubt, to spend it for me on myself was the choice,
As clothes were raffled and sour wine was served, insults were hurled in one great voice.

Those words I did speak, though vain as they were, the choice was mine to make,
Thrust into the air, the sword sliced and cut, and a precious Life it did take.

As if with no warning, the lights they went out, the weather turned rough, and the choice I made was to stop,
A limp body did hang, where once there was life, up above on the mountaintop.

I now saw it so clear, that the choice I did make, to take each step of my life through these times,
Was paid for with a price, so I myself would not die, and suffer for each of my "crimes."

The answer is simple, I'm not in it alone, my life is not my own now I see,
So, from here I will go, with Christ as my guide, His way is The Choice for me.

The Tower

As a youth life's so grand, I'm so young and so free,
nothing can slow me down,
I run like the wind, I go to I go fro, my feet barely touch
the ground.

I'm blown to the things, so fun they do seem, that make me
feel good inside,
The world's so alive, it offers so much, my future looks so
open and wide.

As time marches on, and the years pass me by, I'm given so
much I can choose,
An endless array, placed there on display, there's just no
way I ever will lose.

But experience shows me, through effort and work, there's
still much to learn and to gain,
And though at times the feelings are good, with even some
great, they're wrought in between with some pain.

As the struggles and hurts mount, they may help me to
grow, and teach me a better way to live,
However, they come with a price, as bruised and beat I go
on, and I find I'm beginning to give.

On the outside I'm climbing, the steps towards success, as I
strive for the fame and the power,
But, inside I'm feeling, as though the ascent, has locked me
up high in a Tower.

I'm trapped in this place, no corners to hide, I run like a
dog after its tail,
In search of an answer, that I heard long ago, that says no
matter what, "I can't fail."

As old as the hills, and even beyond, the thought hits my
mind like a cool breeze,
And down I do go, to ask for sure help, and Hope comes as
I go to my knees.

Continuing on, in prayer and fast, those Tower walls they
do crumble and fall,
And I reach high in the air, to the Hand that is there, and I
can again stand mighty and tall.

And so I go through this grand New Life, refreshed as a
youth, where nothing can slow me down,
For the Heavenly Winds carry me on, both to and fro, and
Angel's wings lift me over the ground.

The Road

Traveling down the road of Life, there a beggar chance to be,
Lying in the gutter, in need and want was he.

Dressed in rags, from head to foot, his dirt showed no place clean,
The hungry look, the hollowed cheeks, this man was very lean.

His speech was weak, and not to clear, he mumbled as he spoke,
Some words were foul, some were sincere, he even made a joke.

To passersby he asked for help, he stuck his hand for gifts in the air,
But many turned their heads away, and acted as if they didn't care.

Dumbfounded how he lived his life, I had to ask of his plight,
Not knowing what, that I would hear, or on what it would shed some light.

Conversation began real slow, neither one of us knew what to say,
As no one ever stopped to talk, I brightened up his day.

The words poured out and images formed, the picture became so clear,
This simple man, whose meaning was hid, was placed just for me here.

Understanding flowed from this amazing sight, it surfaced
for me to see and use,
To follow this quiet guidance I received, meant I
couldn't lose.

The rags were useless earthly things, the bad speech and
dirt were from sin,
And no one on earth can give, or feed the hungry look, for
the Great Love desired within.

Because now as I know, lying down in that gutter, that
beggar turned out to be me,
For only God can provide for our every need, as down
The Road of Life go we.

The Carpenter's Son

Designing and creating with gentle hands, the Father instructs the Son,
Teaching and showing Him what He can do, and working until it is done.

The young boy learns how He is to start, and how He's to complete His task,
Growing daily in strength and knowledge of Life, with answers from questions He's asked.

As time marches on, as an age is attained, His wisdom He's ready to spread,
To teach other people of the way they should go, and consequences of which they will dread.

He gathers a group of everyday men, they're called out for all to see,
So no one will feel they're too great or too small, so they know what they too can be.

The low He does reach to pull to their feet, not one will He leave behind,
For the rich and the poor in His eyes are the same, to everyone is He thus kind.

His teachings are straight, He gets to the point, with Love does He show us the way,
What the Father taught Him, He now lets us see, each morning and through each day.

And now well equipped and built to withstand, and shown how to overcome fear,
He prepares us to lead the fight on our own, against forces of those who won't hear.

The battle will rage, look desperate at times, but we must keep up our strong will,
For He promised us Life, when He replaced it with His, up on the Cross on the hill.

Eternity awaits us, into His arms will we go, once our time on the earth does end,
As He goes on before us, a place to prepare, when He's ready for us He will send.

For Heaven was designed and created for us, by gentle hands of the Father and Son,
Who will teach us forever, once and for all, when His eternal Kingdom has come.

The Son That Never Sets

Daily when I wake, the Son is in my eyes,
Brightening my day, to greet me when I rise.

The Son shines as a Light of Hope, to lead me through each day,
With Love and Understanding, to guide me on my way.

Though the road ahead may twist and turn, and slow me for a while,
The Son's Presence glares through it in time, and pulls me through the trial.

So, no worries do I ever have, not long does my mind linger,
As the Son's warm Touch is always there, on my Heart I feel His finger.

And when the day has come and gone, I lay down with no regrets,
For my life is set ablaze each night, as I'm watched over by The Son That Never Sets.

The Letter

One morning I awoke to find, a Letter in my hand,
It stated, "You have been set free, your name is in My Plan."

For years I'd been a captive, from thoughts and actions in my Life,
They seemed to get me further, and be OK, but in the long run caused me strife.

For I kept going down the wrong road, getting deeper as I went,
Till I reached a point so desperate, "My Life's been wasted, not well spent."

Then amidst the dark and dreary Life, that I lead myself into,
I hit the lowest point there was, and a Light came shining through.

I then fell down to my knees, I went to shield the Brightness out,
When a calming Peace came over me, and like a baby I began to pout.

"Please forgive me for the things I've done, I've been wrong and I don't deserve to live,
My whole Life has been a shambles, but it's all I have left to You to give."

These words they seemed so simple, yet so hard they were to say,
Then I found myself ready to sleep, of which had been hard for many a day.

And when I arose and read the Message, to me contained in the Letter,
I saw how the price was paid for my life, and how I could go on forever.

It read, "Trust in the Lord for everything, for He seeks to find all who've been lost,
That's why He gave of Himself, all that He had, and He willingly died on the Cross."

So, when Life gets tough and like a captive you feel, and through these trials it's hard to see,
Just remember to read over "The Letter" again, because Christ's Blood has already set you free.

The Dust On My Cross

Daily I do strive, to overcome the things I do,
I pray, "Lord, please forgive me, for these sins against You."

I know how bad it hurts You, Lord, though I am sometimes rather weak,
But in the end Your Strength, is what I call on and I seek.

For as a tiny human, by myself I need You near,
And You take away my guilt, all my pain and my fear.

You come to me in silence, when I take the time to pray,
All I need is Your assurance, and You brighten up my day.

And when You light my path, and give me Hope to carry on,
I know the enemy's match is met, and together we have won.

So, when I sin and feel real low, and think my Life a loss,
I know for sure, Your Love is there, as I wipe the Dust Off of My Cross.

State of Being

I know I exist, because I AM.
I am true Love expressed, because I AM.

I see Hope for tomorrow, because I AM.
I find comfort in my sorrow, because I AM.

I have courage through my trials, because I AM.
I leave my failures behind in piles, because I AM.

I have Peace in my heart, because I AM.
I give thanks from the start, because I AM.

I will live for eternity beyond, because I AM.
I trust wholly in the Son, because I AM.

I know who I am, because of I AM.

Living In The Lap of Luxury

Searching for success, all my Life I'd spent each hour,
Looking for the wealth, I thought to make me happy give me power.

I threw this time at things I knew would work, the rest I did ignore,
Running after what felt good to me, opening up each and every door.

This pursuit did seem to be rather fun, for a while I would excel,
Till I realized I was empty, inside myself a bone dry well,

Then looking for a drink, to quench the thirst I found I had,
I began to shift my thinking, towards real Joy away from sad.

Moving me to higher ground, my Heart's beat it did increase,
As the Love I felt was all around, I knew it would not cease.

I crawled up in a place so grand, tears flowed out of my eyes,
And all my troubles left from my life, the answers then came to my whys.

So, my Life's searching for success, this time did lead me to discover,
I could be "Living In the Lap of Luxury," in the arms of my Heavenly Father.

God Knows

Life is but a challenge, each and every day we live,
We wonder if we'll make it through, or when our strength will give.

Are we doing the right thing, should we continue with this work,
Or is our effort made in vain, when in the shadows our real gifts lurk?

From out of the dark someone arrives, they're very nice it seems,
Are we going out on a limb for Love, are they someone from our Dreams?

We want for so much more to have, we struggle to get by,
Should we give of what we do not have, we have to wonder why?

Our time we spend is precious yes, where does it seem to go,
Are we using it for what we think, will it give us results to show?

And we know we've wronged, we've crossed the line, we wonder is it too late,
Have we chosen the wrong path in sin, have we chosen our own fate?

Well, the answer to these and other questions, through our Life's challenges we ask each day,
Is a simple and wonderful response, and it will give us Hope and strength anew – God Knows, so Pray.

Who Am I?

"Who Am I?" I have to ask, each day I'm out,
each crowd I face,
It seems as though, I've changed so much,
who I was there is no trace.

There was a time I knew for sure, when I was young,
when I was small,
Now with each turn, I make in Life, someone's bluff,
I have to call.

The world around, expects a lot, it says who I should be,
And now I've gone, so far from home, I can't see the forest
for each tree.

The limb I've climbed to, to please the crowds, has gotten
oh so weak,
The truth of who, I really am, is all I really want to seek.

My search for clues, to my dilemma, I've found as simple,
as a knock on a door,
They are written for me, to read and learn, all the answers, I
am looking for.

From cover to cover, The Book is complete,
it shows me all I need,
On how to live my Life, complete in the Lord, with Who's
Trust and Love I've been freed.

So, the answer of "Who Am I?" it is simple and sweet, and
I will ignore what the world might say,
"I AM A CHILD OF GOD, His Loving Creation Unique,
and I'll proclaim this fact each and every day."

Deep Waters

Standing on the shoreline, looking out across the sea,
I'm in awe of my surroundings, thinking long on
what I can be.

I know my life is special, I was made for something great,
But looking out on the horizon, I feel like I should wait.

So many have gone before me, they've traveled far and
they've gone wide,
As I see the things they've dealt with, fear makes me
want to hide.

The ups and downs, the troubles and trials,
I imagine if it were me,
Can I survive the waves, the winds, the rain,
it's hard for me to see.

At times I've gone so far, my waist was wet,
I've gone up to my chin,
But I've always turned around and ran, to the dry land
did I go in.

I've then pondered my existence, do I really want
to chance it all?
So many voyages in my life have I taken,
so many times I did fall.

Though thinking back in time to those,
who didn't many chances take,
Most later realized their lives were a waste,
they made a big mistake.

And they who dared to rise above, the waves and make
a path,
These were the ones who discovered themselves, and
fulfilled the Dreams they did hath.

Desires of my own do I have within, now I realize where
they come from all along,
We are given these Gifts, from Heaven above, they make us
grow bold and grow strong.

So , now on the shoreline do I stand no more, I'm going
across the sea to what matters,
For I have the Faith and Strength from my Father above,
to conquer this life, I'm challenging the vast Deep Waters.

Still

Still

Quiet

Listen

Cool Refreshing Breeze

Hear THE WORD

Understand the Message

Apply the Knowledge

Love Everyone in All Things

Gain Wisdom

Learn

Teach

Listen

Quiet

Still.

The Two Fisted Fighter

Battle after battle I'd faced each challenge in my life, all alone I had stood up and I had fought,
With my two fists held so tight, I would scrap for every inch, and rejoice in everything that I had got.

For years I'd held my ground, oh so sure I was always right, nothing you could say would change my mind,
And no matter what blocks were thrown, I would figure out a move, in which to get myself out of any bind.

But as my life went on in time, new techniques that I would face, from opponents entering into the ring,
Showed old tricks that I had learned, the tight fists that I'd always used, I began to feel the punches and they'd sting.

After being knocked around, several times I hit the ground, I finally decided in my mind the truth I'd hear,
So on my face I put myself, I opened up my heart to God, and then I asked for His great Love to draw me near.

All the fears I'd held so tight, within my fists now I could see, really only served in my life to hold me back,
For I found true Power in God's Love, He would fight for me instead from high above, each and every time the enemy does attack.

So now each battle I am in, each challenge that I face, I am not alone when I stand up to fight,
For I've unclenched both of my fists, I've opened up my hands to God, and I rejoice in His winning Glory and His might.

The Fools

Life passes by, for each here on earth it's true,
And how that time is spent, is up to both me and you.

One will follow signs, passed down from up above,
The other walks a path, based only on self-love.

Staying in the bounds, written down for all to learn,
Or jumping on ahead, with no thought around each turn.

Guided by a Golden Light, one's future is secure,
As others fall for each flashy sight, and each and every lure.

Faith is all one needs, to move ahead to have success,
And fate becomes the other's way, but always under stress.

Hope comes easy when one trusts, and doors will
open wide,
While terror enters other's lives, and causes them to hide.

One's Life is all full of Love, and ends in the very way that
one will live,
The other gets what is deserved, as much back as
they did give.

So remember, everyone's Life passes by here on earth, each
following certain rules,
And in the end, how that time is spent, both lives will be
labeled as Fools.

Which type of Fool will you be?

The Water

Calm, clean, pure and clear, the Water was fresh and cool,
The sun would shine and warm it each day, as it set in its shallow pool.

Daily the Water enjoyed the peace, and quiet would fill the time,
Watching the trees sway in the wind, with their own rhythm and rhyme.

Early one morning the breeze seemed to stop, as many people did gather around,
The Water was frightened, what did they want, and why did they come to this ground?

They entered the Water in white flowing robes, their faces were sullen and stern,
And they all felt so dirty, more dead than alive, as many waves all around they did churn.

Then one by one they each spoke and were dunked, into the Water they went,
And the words they used sent chills through and through, as each said they did repent.

Every one of these people expressed Trust and Belief, solely in the One up above,
And His presence was felt, through the Water and air, a wonderful feeling of Love.

As the people went forth, renewed as they were, there was Hope now in which to believe,
The Water did too, become alive and refreshed, all the doubt and dirt they did leave.

So, now, once again, the Water lies fresh and clear, but it
views Life in a whole new way,
It's meaning is vast, not shallow and stale, as the Son shines
and warms it each day.

Cross Road

Life is full of twists and turns, there are ups and downs
to drive,
One has to be real watchful, which path to chose
to stay alive.

There is a way that seems right to most, one sees it with
the eyes,
But down beneath the surface deep, a danger lurks and lies.

This is the road of earthly gain, it is short lived with its
treats and pleasures,
Though it falls short of any true value, as it has only rust
and moths as its treasures.

The path of true worth is not seen with one's eyes, it has
only one place to start,
And this is inside where Love can be found, enveloped
within one's Heart.

This Joy and Hope radiates from above, passed down for
each and everyone,
It comes from taking the road less traveled, directly for
God's own Son.

So, choose wisely in Life when faced with a turn, and let
Jesus carry your load,
Let the path that you take, be the only right choice, as you
lay it all down on the
<u>Cross</u> Road.

The Promise

Everyday we come upon travails, that may pull us down,
These are times that can turn each smile we have, into a dreary frown.

As each challenge comes, it makes its mark on all of us it's true,
But how deep an impression it will leave, is up to both me and you.

Most will let it scar their lives, they won't let it change their ways,
Their bitterness grows great with time, and it cuts short their beautiful days.

Then there are those who let the cuts, and extra weight their strength increase,
They carry on despite their burdens, as they know their "New Life" will not cease.

This courage and endurance and faith to move on, is the only simple gesture God asks from us,
As His gift in return, Eternal Life we receive, is His ultimate sign of true Love, He calls it
The Promise.

The Garment

Around each corner I am drawn, into many snares so deep,
It's hard to know what's right or wrong, on what my mind I should keep.

Into each day as I wonder about, my thoughts make me want to know why,
So many others, friends they say, look away as I go by.

And as time creeps along, no crowd in sight, I stare off into the night,
This silence screams so loud that I, am frozen by my plight.

There sitting on the curbside of Life, I feel so low and all run down,
Contemplating these things, seeking the Answer, to turn it back around.

Then along this path the Light does shine, I can see now what I had sought,
My true Treasures are in Faith, Hope and Love, all else is just for naught.

So, I lift up both my hands as I'm sure, that no matter what my trial or its length,
I will give Praise to God's Son, as I grab hold of the hem of His Garment for Strength.

The Swimmer

Currents in my Life keep moving right along,
And Faith in the Lord helps me grow ever strong.

As waves come against me and push me around,
My Anchor and Rock keeps me steady and sound.

When my load drags me down and far off is the shore,
I look for the Lighthouse to guide me once more.

Rough storms may confuse me and blow my eyes
off my goal,
Then His Love will surround me, calm the winds,
rescue my soul.

So, I keep paddling forward in life with no worries
to pull me down,
Knowing my Savior's Hand will be there as He will never
let me drown.

The Christmas Tree

Royal purple was draped so fine at the base, it circled the
Tree as It did stand,
Jutting so straight, up through the air, so perfectly placed
by many a hand.

It was as wide as two arms, stretched far out to each side,
And the limbs were exposed, as if with nothing to hide.

Great spikes were then hammered, to hold everything tight
and in place so well.
Though once up and displayed, no one could see them
or tell.

For It was covered in bright red, all around and to the
ground,
The great Tree was topped off, with one spectacular crown.

And surrounding the Tree, and watching in awe at this
great sight,
Were Shepherds and Angels, praying deep through
the night.

They were lost in the moment, as if time stood still,
weeping for mercy from the pain and the strife,
Then with one great cry, it was all over, and the great Tree
gave up It's beautiful Life.

But fret not my child, this True Christmas Tree is not dead,
as It was planted with real Love in mind,
For three days have passed, new growth has sprung up, and
It is ever green and living in Heaven for us to find.

So, remember, our single source of true growth, happiness
and peace is borne in only one place,
Wrapped tightly in God's loving branches, and in the Light
of His warm loving face.

Perfect

Daily I would strive, to live my life, with no mistake,
Shooting for perfection, to show the world,
get my fair shake.

Working hard, to reach the top, I deserved the very best,
The pressure on, to have it all, to be better than the rest.

Then reality, took its toll, stress mounted and pulled me down,
My once great goal, a fruitless search, had turned my smile into a frown.

Looking deep, within myself, I found no real growth inside,
And I realized, that I was lost, I was on a downward slide.

I hit my knees, to catch my fall, then heard a sound so faint but clear,
"Listen to My Son, He is the way, He gave His Life to lead you here."

My eyes were opened, my heart was filled, I then saw which way to go,
I could never measure up myself, I needed help,
I now did know.

Christ's Life was given, in place of mine, to raise my once lost life to Heaven above,
Wrapped tightly in the arms of God, surrounded always by the best - His Perfect Love.

The King of Rock & Roll

Three glorious years His tour did last, He went throughout the land,
Telling of the Love He brought, with music of a different brand.

Some lyrics were new, others were old, yet all spoke of a peace so great,
Resounding aloud on themes of Joy and Hope, Eternal Life was their defining trait.

All who did listen and believed the Word, their spirits began to fly,
Raising their praises and thank yous to Him, Who sits with The Most High.

But amidst this applause, were some who chose, to close their hearts and ears,
They planned to quiet, His words of Life, so driven by their fears.

Upon a cross they nailed Him high, then they laid Him in a tomb,
This put an end to all His music, there would be no more they did assume.

Then three days later, the earth did shake, bright lights shone from an Angel throng,
The King arose, Rolled back the Rock, and began to sing a whole new song.

"No more will death befall my children, I've broken its
yoke from whence it was tied,
I'm going up to Heaven, to prepare them a place, with the
Father Who is eternally glorified."

Twisted

Gnarled, bent and wind-blown, my Life looks like a mess to see,
But I stand strong in adverse times, just like an ancient Twisted tree.

On gusty shorelines these plants do grow, tempered by trials through time,
And so do I myself commit, traversing a path that may not be sublime.

Along Life's road I'm put to the test, to see just how well that I can adjust,
As are these trees, pushed to the edge, as they weather the storms into which they are thrust.

From out of the night, the rains rush in, but the trees are secure, as their roots have grown deep,
And I myself, may be drenched and feel weak, I know I am safe and I'm sure, I am able to sleep.

My security comes, from my Faith in my Lord, who watches me daily and keeps me from harm,
Just as the trees, stretch proud to the sky, showing the world no need for alarm.

And although these trees look gnarled and blown, and no matter how Twisted that they may be,
They stand strong in rough times, they're firm and secure, just as I am with God's Love for me.

Blind

Why can I not see the pain, I cause when I give in,
To my lusts and lone desires, with my propensity to sin.

At the time, its seems so right, as it makes me feel so good,
If I only knew, the cost of it, if I only understood.

As long ago, the price was paid, so I could be set free,
God, You sent Your only Son, to die here just for me.

A Love so great, He gave His life, an awesome pain
He did endure,
Just so I, could be saved, a heavenly berth for me
He did secure.

To reach this place, streets paved in gold, where my soul
will never perish,
All I have, to do is ask, and Christ will open His arms and
grant my wish.

So, as forgiveness I seek, down on my knees, God pours
out His Grace on me in kind,
And His Heavenly Light, shines through my dark, to open
my Heart once Blind.

The Tree of Life

One Tree amongst the many stood, its beauty outshone
them all,
As time did pass its strength had grown, it was magnificent
and tall.

Many marveled at its power, and loved the shade it gave
beneath,
But some were jealous of it, filled with hate and disbelief.

They cut the Tree one morning, they drove spikes through
its bark and wood,
Then placed it high upon a hill, so all could jeer as they
passed and stood.

Those who loved the Tree were grieved, no words of
comfort could be found,
And once sure the Tree had died, they buried it in
the ground.

Then miracle of wonders, three days had hardly passed by,
That Tree once gone, did sprout again, new growth into
the sky.

The Great News did spread throughout the world, there
would be no more suffering or strife,
As forever will Love and Power abound, from the Fruit of
The Tree of Life.

Nothing But Your Love

I want my life, to matter Lord, to leave this world
a better place,
I know My child, I see your heart, I can read it in your face,

I will climb the highest mountain for You, I will search
deep on the ocean floor,
I believe you will, I'll be there too, even if you go on
a mile more.

I wish to carry others burdens, to make their load a bit
more light,
And when you stumble, I'll lift you too, lend you wings to
help your flight.

I will give to those in need Lord, I will help to ease
their pain,
For this I'll open up My windows, blessings I'll pour out
to you like rain.

And I will give You my whole life, oh Lord, all praise will
go to You above,
I know my child, these things are great, but all I truly want
is Nothing But Your Love.

The Pierced Heart

I opened up my eyes one morning, I thought like any other day,
Unaware what lay ahead for me, or what would come my way.

For I'd always lived just as I pleased, no boundaries did I set,
Till a stranger posed a question deep, one I never will forget.

"Does your heart ache when you stray, do your thoughts drift toward the Cross,
Do you ever wonder about the pain, suffered so your soul would not be a loss?"

He told me my life was not my own, that it was paid for with a price,
And how I lived from this day on, I should consider all my actions twice.

I could picture the nails placed in His hands, I saw on His head the thorny crown,
Then the final blow came into view, when His sword-Pierced Heart dripped blood and water to the ground.

Tears then filled my eyes to think, that it was I who put Him there,
My selfish Life and thoughtless heart, I didn't seem to care.

But now in the morning when I awake, He is the first thought of each new day,
For I know the truth of what lay ahead for me, that He truly is the only way.

The Hill

Running through the streets each day, I work to keep a steady pace,
Training hard to reach my goals, to finish well in each new race.

I set my sights and hit the road, I push to overcome the pain,
But little did I know one day, what on my journey I would gain.

It was just like any other time, so peaceful and calm it did begin,
I was running well and feeling fine, til I heard a voice call to me from within.

I turned to run into the country, as the message said for me to do,
Then it led me to a hillside, where I met with others running too.

Up and around the trail we ran, all together we went in stride,
And everything was going well, til we reached the top of the other side.

We all stopped and stared in wonder, it was such a strange surprise,
For on the Hill was Jesus, nailed to a cross, we couldn't believe our eyes.

I hit my knees and prayed, "Dear God, I know I helped
to put Him there,
But His death means I can be set free, as all my sins does
He have to bare."

Thanking the Lord for the pain He endured, so my life
could be made anew,
I asked for His forgiveness and Love, and a better direction
to run into.

So, now the race I am running, when I hit the streets in
each new day,
Is to set a pace for others and show them, that Jesus truly is
the only way.

The River

Running on a path I'd gone, so many times before,
I came up to a River great, and ran along its shore.

The trip had been real smooth thus far, I was keeping quite a pace,
Til I slipped upon a muddy patch, and fell flat on my face.

Before I could get to my feet, I started sliding down the bank,
I went head first over the side, the swift current gave such a yank.

I struggled hard to fight the drift, I sought to get back to the land,
Each time I thought I had it won, I sank deep into loose sand.

After several lost attempts, my strength and hope were all but gone,
Then I cried a loud for help to come, a greater source to rely upon.

Instantly the water slowed, its level dropped considerably as well,
I found myself able to stand, on a Solid Rock as best I could tell.

My life became much more clear to me, I could see what I had done so wrong,
I fought the currents by myself, and ended up weak instead of strong.

All along my journeys I know, I need much help to see me through,
A dear Friend to call on often, to lift me high when I feel blue.

So now when I am running hard, and my Life sends me a little strife,
I head straight on for the shoreline, and jump into the River of Life.

The Rock

I was wandering lost throughout my Life, until I chanced
to hear,
Of a path that led to a Rock, which would help make things
more clear.

My journey brought me to a narrow trail, that wound its
way around,
Where many others traveled too, at the end this Rock
was found.

I decided to look on awhile, to study how each one saw
the Rock,
And to get a better fix on it, so I sat and listened
to them talk.

One man cursed and spit on it, he was mad with anger in
his face,
But despite this act of hate and rage, the Rock stayed firm
in its place.

Another approached who appeared very wise, but he
tripped as he passed on,
I don't believe he saw the Rock, though it was as clear as
the midday sun.

The next was curious to say the least, he seemed to be
embarrassed and afraid,
Though through it all the Rock was still, listening as long
as the man had stayed.

And then there came a little child, who danced and sang
with glee,
All around and on the Rock, he had no worries and was
most free.

Then I finally got the message that the missing piece to fit
my Life, was found and here at hand,
As I saw now that this path led to victory, and on this Solid
Rock I will forever stand.

The Battle, The War

From every direction, the fire fight is fierce, the smoke rises in the air,
The casualties are many, as the Battle rages on, and lives are being lost everywhere.

The soldiers are striving, to hold the front lines, as the enemy makes advances each day,
But many of the lives, are giving up in droves, they are lost and don't know there is another way.

As their daily lives , spin out of control, the crafty enemy temps of greener grass,
And before they hear the news, that can turn it all around, they give into that which never lasts.

And though many have fallen, and continue to this day, that Good Word still reaches through the dark,
It gives light to those who seek it, it gives the soldiers reason to sing, it all begins from one tiny spark.

Then as this raging fire, of Love and Hope, spreads throughout the land,
More lives will be saved, to fight the good fight, along with the soldiers hand in hand.

So, as each Battle is fought, and though at times it may look rather bleak, hold to the truth down deep inside your core,
And remember when its finished, when the smoke clears from the air, God will stand as victor, for He's already won the War.

Falling On My Face

Each and every morning, I awake to start my day, then
running out the door to join the race,
It doesn't take me long, to end up doing something wrong,
and I seem to end up Falling on My Face.

I strive to do my best, in all the tasks I lay my hands upon,
But gold rarely appears and worse, sometimes the
beauty's gone.

The looks and words from those in charge, or of those who
pass me by,
Is a strange misunderstanding I'm sure, but it all makes me
want to sigh.

For the ones I've reached my hand unto, and had them
turn away,
I cannot have an unkind word, though it sometimes ruins
my day.

And as deep inside my heart I know right, from wrong I
attempt to flee,
My thoughts and actions overcome my will, down again
and again they pull me.

But through all these trials and temptations of Life, I've
come to know one thing that is true,
This being that God Loves those who Love Him, and He
can forgive both me and you.

So, now when I awake with each new day, I remember the
great Gift of God's Grace,
And though I may do many things wrong, I begin it by
Falling On My Face.

The Voice

When I was a child, I listened to the songs, and the calling I received from within,
I would wake with a great wonder, and looking forward to see, where the new adventure would begin.

As time progressed along, and my life took many turns, the noise around me had my mind in tow,
It distracted me from hearing, the words I once had known, and in a new direction I did go.

My life seemed to be going, in a wonderful new place, I really thought that I was right on track,
But an emptiness had filled me, one I could not have described, til I stopped from this new ride and looked back.

In the state of silence, in my motionless advance, I began to recall what I had left behind,
Then in a flood of vast emotion, I began to weep great tears, and I asked for a renewal of my mind.

The experience was awesome, the images became alive, a new freedom and a purpose was so clear,
I would go and spread the News, to those who've turned their volumes down or off, so they too can know the One from which to hear.

So, now, I listen to these songs, as a child again I have become, I've made these instructions my priority of choice,
And this adventure I am on, causes me to wake with great joy, as I anticipate and wait to hear The Voice.

The Edge

Traveling thru Life by the seat of our pants, we think we have it all under control,
We answer to no one enjoying the ride, choosing our way by the dice we roll.

We gamble with chances that give us a rush, it's best to let us pass by,
Nothing can stop us we've got all we need, were on top and flying so high.

But then out of nowhere as if hidden from sight, the end of our road draws near,
Our world starts to crumble as we stammer and stumble, we are suddenly shaken with fear.

We find our self hurling toward places unknown, into weeds and trees thru a hedge,
And before we can stop or slow ourselves down, we find we've gone over The Edge.

In a desperate attempt to be saved from sure death, we cry out for help from above,
Then out of the clouds a Voice rings aloud, "I'm with you My child with My Love."

As we're lifted from harm and our fear fades away, the truth of God's presence becomes clear,
He's always been with us to help with our needs, we just have to ask to draw Him so near.

So, now as we travel thru our life we seek help, we've
given God total control,
For He has the answers to guide and direct our true course,
for His ways are now our real goal.

Shattered

When I was young and life was fresh, I planned my whole course through,
I knew the goals I had to reach, to achieve my dreams and what I'd do.

Everything I did slid in to its place, my future was bright and sure,
All that I would do seemed right, I felt nothing bad could occur.

But as time progressed some valleys were deep, the jagged edged walls I climbed left me battered,
And as I lost my grip on the ropes I was on, all my dreams broke like glass and were Shattered.

I searched for the pieces to gather them up, I now felt hopeless, discouraged and weak,
Then darkness set in making it hard to see, I was lost and knew not which way to seek.

With no farther to fall at the bottom I knelt, I found the Solid Ground for a brand new start,
As I realized the Truth and opened my arms, and asked God to fill the hole in my Heart.

So now as my life is refreshed and renewed, His Passion for me is what I'll pursue,
For He knows what's best as His goals I will strive, the thrill of His Presence is my Dream come true.

Foot Soldiers

Marching off as if to war, ever on the Faithful have trod,
Willing to leave it all behind, giving their whole lives to God.

No sacrifice is too great for them, their minds are geared for Eternal Glory,
Seeking the lost to bring them Home, by telling them of Christ's great story.

He died for their sins once for all, His Blood covers their every offense,
No guilt or shame or wrong that's done, is remembered in any sense.

Their pasts are forgotten and wiped clean, they're once again like white snow,
Simply from asking God for forgiveness, and His Way in which they should go.

Then once they begin their journey of Hope, they too will venture around the earth,
To reach out to those once as they were, to show them of their true worth.

They'll then join in the marching as they travel afar, as ever Faithful servants to those in need,
Feeding and clothing, washing the feet of the weary, as Foot Soldiers who's Lives thru Christ have been freed.

Love's Destiny

Two Hearts created in the Image of God, searching their
whole lives for True Love,
Hoping for the day when their Dreams are fulfilled, praying
consistently to their Father above.

Each Heart was fervent in asking for help, relentlessly
continuing each day,
But time seemed the victor as it slipped on by, alone each
thought they would stay.

As months turned to years and discouragement loomed, the
Two Hearts' Faith remained ever strong,
For both knew their God gracious, He'd answer their calls,
it was only a matter of just how long.

Then one day these Hearts did chance to meet, they knew
from the start each was right,
It was Divine Love working in a Spiritual accord, as from
God's ways they'd never lost sight.

The Two Hearts were then joined as One in the Lord, each
day they give Him all their Praise,
As their Dreams are fulfilled and Hope is still strong,
Love's Destiny remains true in their lives all their days.

Peace

Though the winds, hail, rain, and storms will rage about
and try to cause you strife,
A Peace like a cool summer breeze blows calmly in your
heart and in your life.

As the flood of problems drown you as a river overcoming
its banks to do its worst,
This Peace calms all of your fears like a gentle flowing
stream with living water to quench your every thirst.

Then when your dreams do crumble down as like a dam
that's lost its strength from all of nature's strain,
Peace reassures you your life can be rebuilt and your future
is full of much that you can gain.

Or when the sting of death leaves you alone like a
devastated valley after a great flood has wiped it out,
There is a Peace that brings you comfort and a hope of a
new life full of joy and void of doubt.

And having broken God's Heart as you turned from Him
feeling like a wasteland both barren and bleak,
The Prince of Peace whose Love surpasses all
understanding who gave His Life for yours is there when
you are weak.

The Snowflake

Descending down from Heaven, a snowflake floats alone from above,
Created pure white and unique, it comes to earth full of Hope and Love.

Excited about its adventure, the snowflake joins with many the same,
But soon Life's pressures take over, and it forgets from whence it came.

Hardened thru all its trials, the snowflake becomes dirty and feels so low,
At the bottom and in need of change, it cries out, "Where and to Whom should I go?"

Immediately the Sun emerges, thru the clouds the snowflake sees the brightest ray,
And with the new light to guide it along, it understands the real Truth and the Way.

The warmth and Love it is given, causes the snowflake to thaw and to melt its heart,
It then becomes submerged in a pool of water, its wiped clean and begins a new start.

Then as a vapor the snowflake ascends, no longer alone it goes up through the sky,
Once again as pure white and special, it leaves earth for the Love in Heaven on High.

The Christmas Gift

The search for that perfect Christmas Gift, all through the
land we go each year,
And the true meanings forgotten of the Love, that brought
this day just for us here.

As the very first gift given to us on Christmas day, was
wrapped in swaddling clothes so warm,
It was hard for those who saw this manger scene, to
understand the uniqueness of this tiny form.

When wisdom filled the temple walls, this Gift again
astounded most who heard,
Though just where did this little boy learn so much, it
seemed to some as rather absurd.

Then as the Gift of His teaching filled many hearts, and His
compassion was known all around,
Many followed this Light, which shone for all to see, the
meaning of Life they knew they'd found.

But a few were blinded by selfish intent, this great gift they
would reject,
An end to this nonsense they had to ensure, as His ways
they didn't respect.

One fateful dark day, as bright as it was, the ultimate
Christmas Gift we all then could receive,
Our Eternal lives were assured as the Cross was raised, but
only for those who would believe.

So our search for the perfect Christmas Gift, can be found
throughout the year with ease,
If we remember the True Love that created this day, as we
fall down on our knees.

Shine

Life was rather dull and dark, and I aimlessly wandered all about,
Why was I really here at all, I would question with much doubt.

No purpose did I seem to serve, no one it appeared did care,
From person to person I went and asked, I had gone almost everywhere.

One day an answer was given to me, but not out of the world did it come,
I heard it whispered within my heart, the Holy Spirit is whom it was from.

"You can search the land from coast to coast, but the secret is much more near,
For as a precious Child of God my dear, the Word in you is why you are here."

"Once you've accepted Jesus as Savior, and proclaim Him Lord of your Life,
You become a gift to all you meet, and tell how He overcomes all their strife."

So, now my life is full and bright, I don't wander but have purpose in mind,
As I'm here as a reflection of what's inside, with His Love and Grace do I Shine.

Waves of Wonder

All across the land are blessings spread to those who pray,
Gifts showered down from God on High given each and every day.

His Love is ever present and those who believe in Him are blest,
For as children of the King of Grace we're provided all the best.

We just ask for His forgiveness and welcome Him into our hearts,
And as He offers us Eternal Life all our fear and worry departs.

We then place our Lives in His great care to guide us on our path,
And thank Him for things yet unseen He has for our behalf.

So, as we send up our prayers all across our land roaring loud like thunder,
God on High will shower down His gifts on us in Mighty Waves of Wonder.

The Bridge

Built by a craftsman, the crossbeams were strong,
Raised high in the sky, placed there by a throng.

Iron nails placed thusly, to hold all in its place,
As many stood watching, strange looks on their face.

The outstretched mighty arms, showed that all were now welcome,
Just to follow this new path, no matter where they were from.

And the Gentle Loving hands, were there to hold many,
To fulfill all their dreams, to quell fears if there were any.

Still standing as firmly today, and still leading many to Glory,
The Bridge of Christ Jesus, is the Love that wrote this fine story.

The End From the Beginning

Fretting and worrying, concerned about results our actions make,
Life's twists and turns confuse us much, which path ahead do we take?

If we move too soon, going in directions we have not known,
Can we find our way back, or into problems will we be thrown?

Blocks in the road can drain us down, we can lose our way and ramble,
But financial, spiritual, and our Family's health, are all too precious to gamble.

This is when we lay our lives down, and place it all on the table,
It's where everything changes, for this is when God is most able.

So, no frets, no worries and no concerns, from our actions should we now be having,
As these are all consumed by God's Love, Who knows The End From the Beginning.

Chains

When as a child, I was free as the wind, I spent my time out and I'd roam,
I always knew, as nighttime drew near, I'd find myself safe back at home.

As older I grew, there were challenges new, and farther away I would go,
The paths became cluttered, the burdens increased, I began to grow weary and slow.

To carry this weight, I'd gathered and bagged, had caused me to fall from the top,
And into a valley, I rolled and I tumbled, till I did hit the bottom and stop.

Up on my knees, I looked to the sky, and a simple verse I prayed up above,
Til a hand of assurance, I felt deep in my soul, filled me with warmth and Pure Love.

A voice then spoke to my heart, "As My Child you are free, and no guilt or shame in you remains,
For you've found your way, safe at home in My arms, where I've taken your burdens and loosed all your Chains.

My Plans

I know where I am headed, I know what I am doing, I have my whole life all planned out,
No one can stop me now, I am sure of my success, it's so easy and I have no doubt.

My education's sound, I have just what it takes, I'm in the world to make it big,
And I'll make it to the top, I'm not that far away, all I have to do is scratch and dig.

But wait, something feels wrong, I'm going backwards now, I didn't even see what hit,
As fast as things were here, they suddenly are not, and I've lost complete control of it.

All my dreams have shattered, like glass dropped on the ground, how can I put all the pieces back together,
I need some reassurance, someone to give me help, a Light to help me see through this bad weather.

Then shining through my dark, a loud song rings into my heart, and the answer to my prayer has come unto me,
"Listen always to My voice, I'll lead you where you are to go, for My Plans are what I wish for you to see."

So, now I know I can't be stopped, my success is really sure, and there's no doubt what's up ahead it will be best,
For God knows where I am headed, He knows what I am to do, as my whole life is in His hands and will be blest.

My Back

Daily in my life, I make decisions of what I should do, and then I act,
And many of these times, the paths I choose are not the best, and on God I turn My Back.

As I travel down these roads, misfortune follows along behind, and I feel lost,
Then I stop to look around, I see how far I have strayed off track, and at what cost.

I've wasted so much time, I should have prayed for my advice, and then been still,
Can I ever go back, after I've gone so far away, and be in God's will?

Then I felt God speak to me, His Grace will cover me on days I stray, and in times I lack,
If I put my trust in Him, I know He will be with me everyday, for He's got My Back.

The Unexpected Gift

I've traveled down some roads in life and can say I'm quite ashamed,
And when I look back and see the results they're far from where I aimed.

I shot my mouth off to my parents and wasn't the best as a son,
At times it was much easier to just turn around and run.

The crowd with which I hung at times was questionable at most,
And places I went and things I've seen I'd really rather not boast.

All these instances and others on top over time made me feel so low,
I was at the end of my so-called rope I didn't know where to go.

Then one day I found a friend who explained what to me seemed rather strange.
To turn over my thoughts and my life to God and through this I would see a change.

So I did as he said and a prayer I prayed and a new Light filled my soul and my face,
For no matter my past or where I have come I still received the Unexpected Gift of God's Grace.

The Cross in the Road

The long and winding road of my life has taken me
many places,
As I've journeyed afar from town to town and have seen
a lot of faces.

Several have tried to draw me astray and a few have really
succeeded.
And I've gone off the path I should have been on doing
things I have not needed.

After going to where the darkness reigns and living as if
that was it,
I finally had reached the end of the trail and was ready to
stop and quit.

Then up ahead as I wearied along ready to fall under my
heavy load,
I went up a hill to it's very top and found a Cross
in the road.

I approached very slow, scared and ashamed, of what I
knew I carried with me,
Until I got close and realized the truth, and my eyes where
opened to see.

From this point on my life would be changed and a new
direction I'd take,
And a new world I'd see full of hope and Love as my old
self off I did shake.

So now the long and winding road of my Life, I take is
narrow, focused and clear,
For the purpose of my journeys afar is to lead others to The
Cross in the Road I found here.

What Is It?

What is it that sets the captive hearts free,
Given openly to all to both you and me?

What helps the fallen pick up their lives off the floor,
Open the windows of their souls, unlock the door?

What clears all the clouds and makes gray days clear,
Turns sadness to laughter, makes courage from fear?

What strengthens the weak, gives sight to the blind,
Brings hope to the hopeless, makes one generous and kind?

What is it that gives life to the dead and puts a smile on their face,
My child it's the unending Love of God, it's His great Gift of Grace!

Coming Up From Behind

I always feel like I'm looking ahead from the back,
Running on empty carrying a heavy loaded pack.

I'm in the fast lane yet going nowhere in a hurry,
As all those around me pass by so I start to worry.

I don't understand and feel lost, my life doesn't seem
to matter,
What's it all about, I feel like a whisper amidst
noisy clatter.

A soft Voice I then hear spoken into my heart, a bright
Light that shines so true,
"My child I've already carried your load to Calvary's Hill
and there I died for you!"

"So lay down your burdens, and give Me your hand and
keep Me always first in your heart and mind,
And forever you'll be with Me as by those who reject Me
you'll be Coming Up From Behind."

The Moon

With a look of desperation planted firmly on his face,
A mother asked her son what caused him trouble
in this place.

He looked at her so blankly and said with a deep sigh,
I don't know what I want to be or where to start or try.

I am so small and timid and not the smartest in my class,
And I don't have much to offer as everyone else has.

Then with a great big smile that only a son gets from
his mother,
She told him of his uniqueness and like him there was
no other.

God has made you special and to Him you should ask
your way,
And once you get an answer on His path then you stay.

For Jesus made it plain to us, that He should be our light,
As He shines into our lives to bring sunshine to our night.

A wonderful excitement then suddenly shone out from the
young boy's eyes,
I want to be The Moon he said, so I can reflect the Son into
other's lives.

Those Left Behind

Life on Earth is only a whisper of time, not long do we stay here,
And as sad a commentary that's true, many a one is filled with fear.

"How long do I have?" and "How much can I do?" Before my existence ends,
Keep many awake and wasting their hours, but not one minute it extends.

Their last breathe is fraught with similar words, "If only...", "I should've", and "maybe",
When the thoughts that may have filled their life, could have started out, "Please save me!"

Thanking the Lord for his Love, His dying and Grace, and giving Him all the glory,
Would have brought meaning, joy and a fruitful life, but not have been the end of their story.

For Jesus Himself ensured us all of this fact, to believe in Him and trust in His ways,
We would be given the gift of eternal Life with Him, extending beyond this world's few short days.

So remember, as though many a Life that we knew has come and gone, and they've passed before our eyes,
Our chance is not lost to see them again, if we who are Those Life Behind, would take heed and be wise.

Empty

Empty are the thoughts of those whose minds just drift along,
Weak and worthless do they feel there is no music for a song.

Empty are their Hearts with no melody to fill its void,
Rejected by so many deep inside they are destroyed.

Empty are these lives as all their Hopes are dashed and lost,
How can they go on, what's their answer, what's the cost?

Empty also is the Tomb, the price was paid, their souls can survive,
If they place their Trust in Jesus, for He's Arisen, He's Alive!!

The Path

All journeys through Life begin with a step that carries
you on your way,
And how you choose to point yourself determines where
you end each day.

There are those of you who decide to go and follow the
crowd that's fun you plainly see,
For going this way is fast and wild you are contented and
happy as you can be.

This worldly way is great for a while but eventually the
truth you'll come to know,
That this wide road is laden with death at the end if onward
here you continue to go.

But to allow yourself to be directed down where wise men
have trod in the past,
You will be led along a narrow winding site to where
you're life will always last.

Here is a place where true riches abide where Love and
Forgiveness always are,
Dwelling forever in Heaven above with the bright shining
Morning Star.

So take your steps wisely making them count throughout
life as daily you proceed on your journey,
And choose to point yourself down The Path that will lead
you to be with God for all eternity.

Two Different Ways, Same Mountain

One day as I traveled up the mountainside we call life,
to reach the top of success,
I chanced to pass a man running back down, of what he
spoke I only could guess.

He said a few things I did not understand, for I was focused
on riches and glory,
And I dismissed him and his words as nothing I needed,
and waited not for the end of his story.

I continued on up my goal was the top, nothing would stand
in my way,
But as time passed on by and the journey grew long,
it became hard to tell the night from the day.

Darkness seemed to loom over all that I did, and the paths
were at times very rough,
I fell down several times got lost many too, I felt hopeless
as all had gotten so tough.

Then the clouds seemed to clear as I crested the top of this
hill, I have finally arrived to myself I surmised,
Until I focused my eyes on what stood in my way, I was
utterly ashamedly surprised.

The words of that man who ran by me that day, came
flooding back in to my mind,
And I wondered why I had not heard the truth then, why
had I been so blind.

For up on this hill for the whole world to see, stood three
crosses high up in the air,
Upon the middle hung the Lord Jesus Christ, who died for
me willfully there.

Now I like that man ran real fast down the hill, to tell
everyone of this Living Fountain,
And that although it may seem now we're going
Two Different Ways, we'll all meet on top of this
Same Mountain.

The Temple

The temple was created for the Lord in all His might,
A place for Him to dwell and to outward shine His light.

But some prefer to litter this site as bad choices they do make,
Introducing elements which weaken and corrupt and in partake.

Decay will force the Lord to leave and the structure will be destroyed,
Unless the owner choses to change and a new attitude be employed.

The interior can then be renewed and will be filled with wondrous things,
As the Lord returns and makes strong the walls as Eternal Life He brings.

For the Lord created The Temple with this purpose from the start,
That it be a place for Him to dwell right there inside your Heart.

Streams

Flowing through time with our many thoughts and dreams,
Our lives are guided in ways like the channels of streams.

We begin at the mountaintop in cool running calm brooks,
With no cares in the world all seems peaceful it looks.

But life has its challenges and raging rapids can form,
That throw us all directions like a wild summer storm.

Tossed over the falls without notice into jagged rocks on the valley's floor,
We lose all hope at the bottom with many pains galore.

Then out of our darkness when all seems lost in our eyes,
A bright shining Light reaches into our lives.

The Hands of our Savior evaporates all our cares and our fears,
As He takes us back to the Heavens where there are no tears.

And as time continues to flow we have new thoughts and new dreams,
As our Eternal lives are now directed with God along His Golden Streams.

Like My Father

As day by day time passes by there are many wondrous things I see,
But none come dearer to my Heart than a blessing God gave to me.

The miracle of Life is this gift so full of beauty and so filled with joy,
All wrapped up in this tiny package that I Lovely refer to as, "My Little Boy".

Watching him grow on up so fast each day what touches me like no other,
Is seeing his actions reflecting mine as if to say, "I want to be Like My Father!"

Tears fill my eyes when I see "Daddy's little helper" following so eagerly behind,
So to give him the good and right example to live by myself I continuously remind.

To mirror an image of Love and respect and to reach out to those in need,
Is the way I should live to give him his guidance so he knows how to proceed.

So I myself continue to strive much harder day by day passing the time in reading God's Wondrous Word,
Because I, like my son, want to be Like My Father in Heaven and one day to meet Him I'm looking forward.

God Alone

Some people say there is no God, but I myself have heard
Him speak,
In my Heart, and in my mind, and in the world as
I did seek.

See, I looked other places for my answers in Life, but
nothing else could fill the hole,
That I had deep inside, down where it really matters, to
make me feel more full.

Wandering for years half alive, I came upon a man who
told me finally of a gift,
Of riches beyond measure, wealth none could match, of
One who would close my rift.

He came for one purpose, to set His people free, to release
them from the bondages of sin,
And to ask them to open, their hearts and their lives, and to
simply let Him come in.

So let the gates be unlocked, in your mind and in your soul,
since what you truly seek can be found from no other,
As the inner peace and strength, we all desire deep within,
can come only from Our Father.

And so now those who have ears, in your heart and your
mind, open them so that you can hear,
The words spoken out from Heaven, that God Alone is our
Life, then listen to His Song as He draws near.

The Tree

As a seed in the soil one day I just hoped I would become a great tree,
But little could I have imagined how important my existence for the future would be.

I sprouted in a garden that was so beautiful and inviting so many people ventured through,
A vast array of flowers and vines and pretty trees that I was thrown into.

As time marched on I grew large and tall but never reaching beauty like the rest,
Feeling lost and forgotten in the back of the garden I prayed one day I'd be blest.

Shortly thereafter and several times over the course of three years a young man would visit my shade,
He was strong and sure and spoke wonderful words as prostrate on the ground he laid.

All of His words I kept in my heart and I knew despite what I could see I'd be alright,
Until one day a group of men arrived at my side and began to chop at me with all their might.

The last thing I could hear was how the great strength of my life in my limbs would all become great beams,
To build a cross for that man who visited me and spoke to His Father about His dreams.

Then I finally understood that by giving my life to this "Man" is what really has made me a great tree,
Because by doing so, my very existence paved the way for others to follow Him, He Who died for both you and me.

The Shadow

As I'd made my way through my life I'd almost always
had this feeling,
Of a dark cloud hanging over my head and limitations
like a ceiling.

No matter how hard I did try to rise my best just
didn't cut it,
I always fell down to the ground it seemed to crush
my spirit.

I struggled to my feet each time and found
new things to do,
Though I kept on sliding back far more and was about
to say, "I'm through."

But while lying on my face this time I heard a voice speak
to my Heart and say,
"You've done things on your own too long, I have
a better way."

"Put your past behind you leave your cares and worries and
follow Me,
I will be the strength you need as a fresh new life I will
give to thee."

So I looked up to the Heavens on high and spoke a
simple prayer,
I asked the Lord into my Heart and then felt Him
enter there.

Tears of joy filled both my eyes and I knew I no longer had to be the best,
For by placing my life and trust in the Lord in Him I would also rest.

So, now as I walk on through my life if I am drained or feeling low,
Straight into The Shadow of His Love and to the Fruits of His Spirit I will go!

Is It I?

Is it I, Lord, who condemned You, who drove You
to Your fate,
Did I not fail to listen to Your Word, for me is it too late?

Is it I, Lord, who scourged You with the whip, making You
bleed so,
Did I not lash out at my brother, where is it can I now go?

Is it I, Lord, who placed the crown of thorns, on top of Your
dear head,
Did I not heap a burden on my neighbor, how is it I turned
my back instead?

Is it I, Lord, who pierced the nails, who did pound them
through Your feet and hands,
Did I not utter sharp remarks in hate, what is it of me Your
Law demands?

Is it I, Lord, who placed You on the cross, who caused You
to breathe Your last,
Did I not deny knowing You to others, who is it that can
forgive my past?

It is You, Lord, Who died for me, You Who gave for mine
Your Life's breath,
I did not deserve this Graceful gift, but I accepted it in my
heart by Faith.

The Rose

The beauty of the Rose is known the whole of the world around,
And to receive this gift in Love not much greater can be found.

Great care is taken to grow them right from when they are first born,
Until they're full in bloom arrayed on their long stem filled with the thorn.

When One is pierced great suffering ensues and also there is great pain,
But the Bouquet of Glory that's set on High in the end becomes the gain.

As such, Jesus chose to be crucified and He died for the world, His gift for us He made in Love,
And then Christ Rose, the most beautiful one through time, for us to join Him in Heaven forever above.

God's Wondrous Love

God's so full of love it's true, and He wants to show
it to us,
So He thought He'd express it out so grand, and He made
this great big fuss.

Across the earth He made great sites, He formed them
from the land,
But some were not impressed with these, that they were not
so grand.

He then spread the sky from east to west, with stars with
beauty bright,
Again many only looked away, as if they were not
such a site.

So He looked long and hard into our hearts, and thought
that hey just maybe,
The best way we could see God's Wondrous Love, would
be expressed in a tiny baby.

New Life

The blackness of the nights gave way to even darker days,
As the clouds of despair remained in my life creating such a haze.

Gloomy thoughts rained hard in my mind as I drowned in such a sorrow,
And I knew unless a lifeboat was sent I had no real hope for tomorrow.

As I began to feel myself sinking away I gave a gasp with my last breath,
I spoke a simple prayer for help and I was suddenly snatched from death.

I was told my past was washed anew and I set sail on a whole new course,
One in which the skies remain clear with an everlasting Light source.

And so now no clouds can cover up my days for all is bright and sunny ahead,
As the shadows of night have been cast away and a New Life do I have instead.

One

Two separate lives wandering alone, on different paths they both did go,
Though deep inside each felt the same, just like they were not whole.

Each tried to fit some pieces in place, to make their lives complete,
But no matter which way they pushed or pulled, the pictures looked far from neat.

After several years of prayer and patience, each began to focus more clear,
God's preparations for them were complete, and to each other He brought them near.

With God at the helm it was love at first sight, each knew it was right from the start,
And they came together as Husband and Wife, never again would they be apart.

So now they travel along the same path, hand in hand with God as their guide,
For the two halves they once had been, have become One Heart down deep inside.

Threads

Woven throughout the history of time, all things are tied together as one,
And into the future the seams will be sewn, until the story is done.

As if a fairy tale it began, all was good and perfect to see,
Until a shadow was cast abroad, it would mean death to all there would be.

A way was made to wash this completely a way, to cover it up so deep,
But stubbornness caused it to surface again, back into the world it did seep.

Confusion ensued and all scattered abroad, to separate out wheat from the chaff,
Then soon One was prophesied to come and to save, by peace and not from the staff.

On a cold winters morn a baby was born, True Love came to live with us here,
And from that moment all lives would be changed, we no longer would live in fear.

The Word would spread both far and wide, It came among us to set us free,
Until one fateful but joyous Spring day, when we hung Him on a tree.

Our sorrow soon turned into singing and dancing, once three days did pass on by,
As our Savior and Redeemer He did rise, and went up to His place on High.

And now we await His returning, His glorious
announcement as He is trumpeted in,
For the next time He comes in a chariot, and with fire He
will destroy our sin.

So, remember to learn from our past, and how God weaves
all things for His Glory,
And see if you can find yourself in His Threads, and
become a part of His story.

No More Silence

Alone and afraid Jesus' Disciples were there, hidden away in the upper room,
For it was only a short time that day was past, and all were filled with such gloom.

They hadn't quite grasped as yet the cross, and just why the Lord had to die,
Just sitting and praying, awaiting some news, asking each other why.

Then through the wall there Jesus did stand, right in front of their eyes,
And later with many together as one, when into the Heavens He did rise.

He spoke to them thusly that He must return, back to His Father above,
But with them He'd leave a Guide to go on, a wonderful gift of His Love.

The Holy Spirit then did come unto them, a flame of fire to charge each soul,
One who would speak to their hearts and direct their ways, as into the world they would go.

Many people did they see and go to with the Word, those who were lost and filled with strife,
To spread the Good News that Jesus is Lord, to believe in Him would save their life.

Two thousand years have passed on by, but the message remains the same,
That Eternal Life can be yours too, if only you'd call on His Name.

So, if you feel you're alone with gloom in your life, and you have hidden yourself far away,
Just call on Jesus to enter your life, and No More Silence will be, as He speaks to your heart today.

No Strings

Not many want to give away the things that they've possessed,
Be it time or gifts or money except for a return where they are blest.

They are in it for the glory for a name or some control,
To call the shots with their own hands self-sufficiency is their goal.

But most all do find the strain is great to traverse alone in Life,
That in the end the load they've packed only makes the way for strife.

Heavy laden and trudging along they reach out for some relief,
Though many will ask most will wither away due to lack of a belief.

For to understand the Help's real nature they must see with the eyes of their heart,
And learn to dig deep for the truth to tell earthly things and Heaven's apart.

Answers will reveal an invisible Hand orchestrating Life's music that we hear,
It guides us too on through our life though no force is given to us to adhere.

We were created in His image to follow His ways but like puppets we are not,
As He gave us the freedom with No Strings attached on our own we must choose our lot.

In the end our choice is simple and sure but He doesn't throw it up in our face,
For Christ freely gave His Life for our own we need only accept His Saving Grace.

The Crown

Adorned in jewels beyond compare its beauty outshines them all,
The crown which was placed upon His head was first shocking to those who saw.

For it glistened from the Son's bright red colors which then reflected His Light,
As the sharp thorns woven into its mesh were forced onto His head with such might.

"Why would our "King" allow such a thing and why did He endure this pain?"
Well, the message was shown in time it was clear His ordeal became our gain.

For He suffered and died and took upon Himself all the guilt and shame of our sin,
Then as three days did pass the Word took new life as He did arise once again.

He was transformed as He ascended on High and His crown it too became new,
Because once in Christ all are redeemed even those who seem so ordinary like me and you.

So, place yourself firm in Christ's loving hands and despite your past He'll turn your life around,
As His free gift of Grace adorns us in His beautiful Light and we receive Our Crown.

The Sea

Born into a world meant for our joy that's full of beauty and for life,
We wade into the sea of human suffering caused by sin that gives us strife.

The weight of our Life's daily burdens overloads our hearts and tends to pull us down,
And most for lack of a safety net succumb to this and do hopelessly then drown.

For each and every one of us there however is a Hand of Hope that reaches out and through the mist,
He is the One Who walks upon the water He created to rescue us and add us to His list.

Our choice is simple to be included thus we need merely respond and place our lives in His hands,
As He has already parted the waters between Life and Death showing us of His Eternal Plans.

So, though in this world The Sea be vast as far as east is from west we are His once reborn,
We are saved from our sins by His death then to Life and from His side never again shall be torn.

When Lines Blur

God's ways are not like ours, His standards are the best,
To stray off of the course He sets, turns our lives
into a mess.

We think we can tell right from wrong, on our own outside
His Word,
But this only shades us from His Truth, and is
utterly absurd.

For God sees things in black and white, there is good and
there is bad.
No patterns are there in the gray, no in-betweens
will be had.

As sin infects our lives on earth, changes in our hearts
can occur,
And we take our eyes off of God's Laws, and that is
When Lines Blur.

However God is Love above all else, and once again He'll
draw us near,
Simply place our Trust in Him alone, and our directions
will become more clear.

Then what once was a mess will be made straight, from His
course we will not stray,
And we'll understand that He knows best, and that His way
is the only way.

Lost In Translation

God placed us in a Paradise and left us with His Word,
But we turned our heads away from Him as if
we'd never heard.

For some time again we listened, raised our kids and
farmed the mud,
However the values were not passed along so God sent to
us the Flood.

He washed away most of the evil as He showed us His
Great Power,
Once again though we did stray away trusting ourselves
and building a tower.

Cast into confusion, Babeling senseless we were strewn out
to every nation,
As we could not understand our brothers words, since they
were again Lost in Translation.

Christ then did come to explain the Word and show us of
our impending loss,
Yet once again we looked the other way and we hung Him
on the Cross.

Two thousand years have come and gone since Christ went
before us to set the future stage,
And many still forget the past and stray and have failed to
add their names to His great page.

So, if we just simply turn our eyes upon Him, learn His
Word and take His advice,
God will once again see favor in us and invite us back into
His Paradise.

Seeds

God makes each of us special, no other like us is there,
And inside He has placed talents, for future fruits
we can bear.

Our goal is quite very simple, to discover these strengths
deep within,
To fulfill our true purpose, to allow miracles from Him
to begin.

We start out on the journey He's set, spreading His seeds of
Faith and of Love,
With our hands left outstretched, open for others and for
God's gifts from above.

Patience will yield in due time, much more than we
ourselves could create,
A Harvest so vast and so large, it's a testament to our God
He is great.

And though the workers are few, the bountiful blessings in
time we will reap,
As we stay true and straight to His path, and the words of
His Book do we keep.

So, find out how you're God's unique creation, and how
wonderfully made you are,
Then let His Light that's inside you shine out, as you spread
your Seeds both wide and far.

Printed in the United States
79705LV00002B/199-1500